This record book belongs

School _____   Pho

Grade _____   Room _____   Year _____

MW01201663

Contents

Record student names across the top.

Record dates of assessments or use a section for each quarter of the year.

Record individual proficiencies at each date. You may choose to use any system, such as check marks, a 1–4 rubric, letters, or grades.

	Cara Avery				Luis Diaz				Sam Edwards				Jayl	
	9/6	9/8	10/15	2/3	9/6	9/8	10/15	2/3	9/6	9/8	10/15	2/3	9/6	9/
3.OA.A.1	1	1	2	2	3	3	3	4	1	2	2	3	2	3
	– struggles with interpreting products of whole numbers				– successful with interpreting products of whole numbers				– needs help expressing the product in a context				– strugg multipl	

Add detailed notes throughout the year.

For a more comprehensive resource guide with tips and additional reproducibles, visit *activities.carsondellosa.com*.

Printed in the USA • All rights reserved.

ISBN 978-1-4838-1114-7
01-135147784

Math Standards At a Glance

Represent and solve problems involving multiplication and division.
3.OA.A.1 Interpret products of whole numbers.
3.OA.A.2 Interpret whole-number quotients of whole numbers.
3.OA.A.3 Use multiplication and division within 100 to solve word problems in situations involving equal groups, arrays, and measurement quantities.
3.OA.A.4 Determine the unknown whole number in a multiplication or division equation relating three whole numbers.

Understand properties of multiplication and the relationship between multiplication and division.
3.OA.B.5 Apply properties of operations as strategies to multiply and divide.
3.OA.B.6 Understand division as an unknown-factor problem.

Multiply and divide within 100.
3.OA.C.7 Fluently multiply and divide within 100, using strategies such as the relationship between multiplication and division or properties of operations. By the end of Grade 3, know from memory all products of two one-digit numbers.

Solve problems involving four operations, and identify and explain patterns in arithmetic.
3.OA.D.8 Solve two-step word problems using the four operations. Represent these problems using equations with a letter standing for the unknown quantity. Assess the reasonableness of answers using mental computation and estimation strategies including rounding.
3.OA.D.9 Identify arithmetic patterns (including patterns in the addition table or multiplication table), and explain them using properties of operations.

Use place value understanding and properties of operations to perform multi-digit arithmetic.
3.NBT.A.1 Use place value understanding to round whole numbers to the nearest 10 or 100.
3.NBT.A.2 Fluently add and subtract within 1000 using strategies and algorithms based on place value, properties of operations, and/or the relationship between addition and subtraction.
3.NBT.A.3 Multiply one-digit whole numbers by multiples of 10 in the range 10–90 using strategies based on place value and properties of operations.

Develop understanding of fractions as numbers.
3.NF.A.1 Understand a fraction 1/*b* as the quantity formed by 1 part when a whole is partitioned into *b* equal parts; understand a fraction *a/b* as the quantity formed by a parts of size 1/*b*.
3.NF.A.2 Understand a fraction as a number on the number line; represent fractions on a number line diagram.
 3.NF.A.2a Represent a fraction 1/*b* on a number line diagram by defining the interval from 0 to 1 as the whole and partitioning it into b equal parts. Recognize that each part has size 1/*b* and that the endpoint of the part based at 0 locates the number 1/*b* on the number line.
 3.NF.A.2b Represent a fraction *a/b* on a number line diagram by marking off a lengths 1/*b* from 0. Recognize that the resulting interval has size *a/b* and that its endpoint locates the number *a/b* on the number line.

3.NF.A.3 Explain equivalence of fractions in special cases, and compare fractions by reasoning about their size.
 3.NF.A.3a Understand two fractions as equivalent (equal) if they are the same size, or the same point on a number line.
 3.NF.A.3b Recognize and generate simple equivalent fractions. Explain why the fractions are equivalent.
 3.NF.A.3c Express whole numbers as fractions, and recognize fractions that are equivalent to whole numbers.
 3.NF.A.3d Compare two fractions with the same numerator or the same denominator by reasoning about their size. Recognize that comparisons are valid only when the two fractions refer to the same whole. Record the results of comparisons with the symbols >, =, or <, and justify the conclusions.

Note: Grade 3 expectations in this domain are limited to fractions with denominators 2, 3, 4, 6 and 8.

Solve problems involving measurement and estimation of intervals of time, liquids, volumes, and masses of objects.
3.MD.A.1 Tell and write time to the nearest minute and measure time intervals in minutes. Solve word problems involving addition and subtraction of time intervals in minutes.
3.MD.A.2 Measure and estimate liquid volumes and masses of objects using standard units of grams (g), kilograms (kg), and liters (l). Add, subtract, multiply, or divide to solve one-step word problems involving masses or volumes that are given in the same units.

Represent and interpret data.
3.MD.B.3 Draw a scaled picture graph and a scaled bar graph to represent a data set with several categories. Solve one- and two-step "how many more" and "how many less" problems using information presented in scaled bar graphs.
3.MD.B.4 Generate measurement data by measuring lengths using rulers marked with halves and fourths of an inch. Show the data by making a line plot, where the horizontal scale is marked off in appropriate units—whole numbers, halves, or quarters.

Geometric measurement: understand concepts of area and relate area to multiplication and to addition.

3.MD.C.5 Recognize area as an attribute of plane figures and understand concepts of area measurement.

3.MD.C.5a A square with side length 1 unit, called "a unit square," is said to have "one square unit" of area, and can be used to measure area.

3.MD.C.5b A plane figure which can be covered without gaps or overlaps by n unit squares is said to have an area of n square units.

3.MD.C.6 Measure areas by counting unit squares (square cm, square m, square in, square ft, and improvised units).

3.MD.C.7 Relate area to the operations of multiplication and addition.

3.MD.C.7a Find the area of a rectangle with whole-number side lengths by tiling it, and show that the area is the same as would be found by multiplying the side lengths.

3.MD.C.7b Multiply side lengths to find areas of rectangles with whole-number side lengths in the context of solving real world and mathematical problems, and represent whole-number products as rectangular areas in mathematical reasoning.

3.MD.C.7c Use tiling to show in a concrete case that the area of a rectangle with whole-number side lengths a and $b + c$ is the sum of $a \times b$ and $a \times c$. Use area models to represent the distributive property in mathematical reasoning.

3.MD.C.7d Recognize area as additive. Find areas of rectilinear figures by decomposing them into non-overlapping rectangles and adding the areas of the non-overlapping parts, applying this technique to solve real world problems.

Geometric measurement: understand perimeter as an attribute of plane figures and distinguish between linear and area measures.

3.MD.D.8 Solve real world and mathematical problems involving perimeters of polygons, including finding the perimeter given the side lengths, finding an unknown side length, and exhibiting rectangles with the same perimeter and different areas or with the same area and different perimeters.

Reason with shapes and their attributes.

3.G.A.1 Understand that shapes in different categories may share attributes, and that the shared attributes can define a larger category. Recognize rhombuses, rectangles, and squares as examples of quadrilaterals, and draw examples of quadrilaterals that do not belong to any of these subcategories.

3.G.A.2 Partition shapes into parts with equal areas. Express the area of each part as a unit fraction of the whole.

Language Arts Standards At a Glance

Key Ideas and Details

RL.3.1 Ask and answer questions to demonstrate understanding of a text, referring explicitly to the text as the basis for the answers.

RL.3.2 Recount stories, including fables, folktales, and myths from diverse cultures; determine the central message, lesson, or moral and explain how it is conveyed through key details in the text.

RL.3.3 Describe characters in a story and explain how their actions contribute to the sequence of events.

Craft and Structure

RL.3.4 Determine the meaning of words and phrases as they are used in a text, distinguishing literal from nonliteral language.

RL.3.5 Refer to parts of stories, dramas, and poems when writing or speaking about a text, using terms such as chapter, scene, and stanza; describe how each successive part builds on earlier sections.

RL.3.6 Distinguish their own point of view from that of the narrator or those of the characters.

Integration of Knowledge and Ideas

RL.3.7 Explain how specific aspects of a text's illustrations contribute to what is conveyed by the words in a story.

RL.3.8 (not applicable to literature)

RL.3.9 Compare and contrast the themes, settings, and plots of stories written by the same author about the same or similar characters.

Range of Reading and Level of Text Complexity

RL.3.10 By the end of the year, read and comprehend literature, including stories, dramas, and poetry, at the high end of the grades 2–3 text complexity band independently and proficiently.

Language Arts Standards At a Glance

RI

Key Ideas and Details
RI.3.1 Ask and answer questions to demonstrate understanding of a text, referring explicitly to the text as the basis for the answers.

RI.3.2 Determine the main idea of a text; recount the key details and explain how they support the main idea.

RI.3.3 Describe the relationship between a series of historical events, scientific ideas or concepts, or steps in technical procedures in a text, using language that pertains to time, sequence, and cause/effect.

Craft and Structure
RI.3.4 Determine the meaning of general academic and domain-specific words and phrases in a text relevant to a *grade 3 topic or subject area*.

RI.3.5 Use text features and search tools to locate information relevant to a given topic efficiently.

RI.3.6 Distinguish their own point of view from that of the author of a text.

Integration of Knowledge and Ideas
RI.3.7 Use information gained from illustrations and the words in a text to demonstrate understanding of the text.

RI.3.8 Describe the logical connection between particular sentences and paragraphs in a text.

RI.3.9 Compare and contrast the most important points and key details presented in two texts on the same topic.

Range of Reading and Level of Text Complexity
RI.3.10 By the end of the year, read and comprehend informational texts, including history/social studies, science, and technical texts, at the high end of the grades 2–3 text complexity band independently and proficiently.

RF

Phonics and Word Recognition
RF.3.3 Know and apply grade-level phonics and word analysis skills in decoding words.

    RF.3.3a Identify and know the meaning of the most common prefixes and derivational suffixes.

    RF.3.3b Decode words with common Latin suffixes.

    RF.3.3c Decode multisyllable words.

    RF.3.3d Read grade-appropriate irregularly spelled words.

Fluency
RF.3.4 Read with sufficient accuracy and fluency to support comprehension.

    RF.3.4a Read grade-level text with purpose and understanding.

    RF.3.4b Read grade-level prose and poetry orally with accuracy, appropriate rate, and expression on successive readings.

    RF.3.4c Use context to confirm or self-correct word recognition and understanding, rereading as necessary.

W

Text Types and Purposes
W.3.1 Write opinion pieces on topics or texts, supporting a point of view with reasons.

    W.3.1a Introduce the topic or text they are writing about, state an opinion, and create an organizational structure that lists reasons.

    W.3.1b Provide reasons that support the opinion.

    W.3.1c Use linking words and phrases to connect opinion and reasons.

    W.3.1d Provide a concluding statement or section.

W.3.2 Write informative/explanatory texts to examine a topic and convey ideas and information clearly.

    W.3.2a Introduce a topic and group related information together; include illustrations when useful to aiding comprehension.

    W.3.2b Develop the topic with facts, definitions, and details.

    W.3.2c Use linking words and phrases to connect ideas within categories of information.

    W.3.2d Provide a concluding statement or section.

W.3.3 Write narratives to develop real or imagined experiences or events using effective technique, descriptive details, and clear event sequences.

    W.3.3a Establish a situation and introduce a narrator and/or characters; organize an event sequence that unfolds naturally.

    W.3.3b Use dialogue and descriptions of actions, thoughts, and feelings to develop experiences and events or show the response of characters to situations.

    W.3.3c Use temporal words and phrases to signal event order.

    W.3.3d Provide a sense of closure.

Production and Distribution of Writing
W.3.4 With guidance and support from adults, produce writing in which the development and organization are appropriate to task and purpose.

W.3.5 With guidance and support from peers and adults, develop and strengthen writing as needed by planning, revising, and editing.

W.3.6 With guidance and support from adults, use technology to produce and publish writing as well as to interact and collaborate with others.

Research to Build and Present Knowledge
W.3.7 Conduct short research projects that build knowledge about a topic.

W.3.8 Recall information from experiences or gather information from print and digital sources; take brief notes on sources and sort evidence into provided categories.

W.3.9 (begins in grade 4)

Range of Writing
W.3.10 Write routinely over extended time frames and shorter time frames for a range of discipline-specific tasks, purposes, and audiences.

Comprehension and Collaboration

SL.3.1 Engage effectively in a range of collaborative discussions with diverse partners on *grade 3 topics and texts*, building on others' ideas and expressing their own clearly.

    SL.3.1a Come to discussions prepared, having read or studied required material; explicitly draw on that preparation and other information known about the topic to explore ideas under discussion.

    SL.3.1b Follow agreed-upon rules for discussions.

    SL.3.1c Ask questions to check understanding of information presented, stay on topic, and link their comments to the remarks of others.

    SL.3.1d Explain their own ideas and understanding in light of the discussion.

SL.3.2 Determine the main ideas and supporting details of a text read aloud or information presented in diverse media and formats, including visually, quantitatively, and orally.

SL.3.3 Ask and answer questions about information from a speaker, offering appropriate elaboration and detail.

Presentation of Knowledge and Ideas

SL.3.4 Report on a topic or text, tell a story, or recount an experience with appropriate facts and relevant, descriptive details, speaking clearly at an understandable pace.

SL.3.5 Create engaging audio recordings of stories or poems that demonstrate fluid reading at an understandable pace; add visual displays when appropriate to emphasize or enhance certain facts or details.

SL.3.6 Speak in complete sentences when appropriate to task and situation in order to provide requested detail or clarification.

Conventions of Standard English

L.3.1 Demonstrate command of the conventions of standard English grammar and usage when writing or speaking.

    L.3.1a Explain the function of nouns, pronouns, verbs, adjectives, and adverbs in general and their functions in particular sentences.

    L.3.1b Form and use regular and irregular plural nouns.

    L.3.1c Use abstract nouns.

    L.3.1d Form and use regular and irregular verbs.

    L.3.1e Form and use the simple verb tenses.

    L.3.1f Ensure subject-verb and pronoun-antecedent agreement.

    L.3.1g Form and use comparative and superlative adjectives and adverbs, and choose between them depending on what is to be modified.

    L.3.1h Use coordinating and subordinating conjunctions.

    L.3.1i Produce simple, compound, and complex sentences.

L.3.2 Demonstrate command of the conventions of standard English capitalization, punctuation, and spelling when writing.

    L.3.2a Capitalize appropriate words in titles.

    L.3.2b Use commas in addresses.

    L.3.2c Use commas and quotation marks in dialogue.

    L.3.2d Form and use possessives.

    L.3.2e Use conventional spelling for high-frequency and other studied words and for adding suffixes to base words.

    L.3.2f Use spelling patterns and generalizations in writing words.

    L.3.2g Consult reference materials, including beginning dictionaries, as needed to check and correct spellings.

Knowledge of Language

L.3.3 Use knowledge of language and its conventions when writing, speaking, reading, or listening.

    L.3.3a Choose words and phrases for effect.

    L.3.3b Recognize and observe differences between the conventions of spoken and written standard English.

Vocabulary Acquisition and Use

L.3.4 Determine or clarify the meaning of unknown and multiple-meaning word and phrases based on *grade 3 reading and content*, choosing flexibly from a range of strategies.

    L.3.4a Use sentence-level context as a clue to the meaning of a word or phrase.

    L.3.4b Determine the meaning of the new word formed when a known affix is added to a known word.

    L.3.4c Use a known root word as a clue to the meaning of an unknown word with the same root.

    L.3.4d Use glossaries or beginning dictionaries, both print and digital, to determine or clarify the precise meaning of key words and phrases.

L.3.5 Demonstrate understanding of figurative language, word relationships and nuances in word meanings.

    L.3.5a Distinguish the literal and nonliteral meanings of words and phrases in context.

    L.3.5b Identify real-life connections between words and their use.

    L.3.5c Distinguish shades of meaning among related words that describe states of mind or degrees of certainty.

L.3.6 Acquire and use accurately grade-appropriate conversational, general academic, and domain-specific words and phrases, including those that signal spatial and temporal relationships.

Operations and Algebraic Thinking

3.OA.A.1 Interpret products of whole numbers, e.g., interpret 5 times; 7 as the total number of objects in 5 groups of 7 objects each. *For example, describe a context in which a total number of objects can be expressed as 5 × 7.*

3.OA.A.2 Interpret whole-number quotients of whole numbers, e.g., interpret 56 ÷ 8 as the number of objects in each share when 56 objects are partitioned equally into 8 shares, or as a number of shares when 56 objects are partitioned into equal shares of 8 objects each. *For example, describe a context in which a number of shares or a number of groups can be expressed as 56 ÷ 8.*

3.OA.A.3 Use multiplication and division within 100 to solve word problems in situations involving equal groups, arrays, and measurement quantities, e.g., by using drawings and equations with a symbol for the unknown number to represent the problem.

3.OA.A.4 Determine the unknown whole number in a multiplication or division equation relating three whole numbers. *For example, determine the unknown number that makes the equation true in each of the equations 8 × ? = 48, 5 = ❑ ÷ 3, 6 × 6 = ?*

3.OA.B.5 Apply properties of operations as strategies to multiply and divide. *Examples: If × 4 = 24 is known, then 4 × 6 = 24 is also known. (Commutative property of multiplication.) 3 × 5 × 2 can be found by 3 × 5 = 15, then 15 × 2 = 30, or by 5 × 2 = 10, then 3 × 10 = 30. (Associative property of multiplication.) Knowing that 8 × 5 = 40 and 8 × 2 = 16, one can find 8 × 7 as 8 × (5 + 2) = (8 × 5) + (8 × 2) = 40 + 16 = 56. (Distributive property.)*

3.OA.B.6 Understand division as an unknown-factor problem. *For example, find 32 ÷ 8 by finding the number that makes 32 when multiplied by 8.*

3.OA.C.7 Fluently multiply and divide within 100, using strategies such as the relationship between multiplication and division (e.g., knowing that 8 × 5 = 40, one knows 40 ÷ 5 = 8) or properties of operations. By the end of Grade 3, know from memory all products of two one-digit numbers.

3.OA.D.8 Solve two-step word problems using the four operations. Represent these problems using equations with a letter standing for the unknown quantity. Assess the reasonableness of answers using mental computation and estimation strategies including rounding. *(This standard is limited to problems posed with whole-numbers and having whole-number answers.)*

3.OA.D.9 Identify arithmetic patterns (including patterns in the addition table or multiplication table), and explain them using properties of operations. *For example, observe that 4 times a number is always even, and explain why 4 times a number can be decomposed into two equal addends.*

Standards Crosswalk

Second Grade

Operations and Algebraic Thinking

Represent and solve problems involving addition and subtraction.
- Use addition and subtraction within 100 to solve one- and two-step word problems with unknowns in all positions (including those represented by a symbol).

Add and subtract within 20.
- Fluently add and subtract within 20 using mental strategies.
- Memorize all sums of two one-digit numbers.

Work with equal groups of objects to gain foundations for multiplication.
- Determine if a group of up to 20 objects represents an odd or even number.
- Use addition to find the total number of objects arranged in rectangular arrays with up to five rows and up to five columns.
- Write an equation to express the sum of an array.

Fourth Grade

Operations and Algebraic Thinking

Use the four operations with whole numbers to solve problems.
- Interpret a multiplication equation as a comparison.
- Multiply or divide to solve word problems involving multiplicative comparison.
- Solve multistep word problems involving whole numbers using the four operations, including problems in which remainders must be interpreted.
- Represent multi-step word problems using equations with a variable.

Gain familiarity with factors and multiples.
- Find all factor pairs for a whole number in the range 1–100.
- Understand that a whole number is a multiple of each of its factors.
- Determine whether a given whole number in the range 1–100 is prime or composite.

Generate and analyze patterns.
- Generate a number or shape pattern that follows a given rule.

3.OA.A.1																				
3.OA.A.2																				
3.OA.A.3																				
3.OA.A.4																				
3.OA.B.5																				
3.OA.B.6																				
3.OA.C.7																				
3.OA.D.8																				
3.OA.D.9																				

8

© Carson-Dellosa CD-104802

3.OA.A.1																				
3.OA.A.2																				
3.OA.A.3																				
3.OA.A.4																				
3.OA.B.5																				
3.OA.B.6																				
3.OA.C.7																				
3.OA.D.8																				
3.OA.D.9																				

3.OA.A.1					
3.OA.A.2					
3.OA.A.3					
3.OA.A.4					
3.OA.B.5					
3.OA.B.6					
3.OA.C.7					
3.OA.D.8					
3.OA.D.9					

Number and Operations in Base Ten

3.NBT.A.1

Use place value understanding to round whole numbers to the nearest 10 or 100.

3.NBT.A.2

Fluently add and subtract within 1000 using strategies and algorithms based on place value, properties of operations, and/or the relationship between addition and subtraction.

3.NBT.A.3

Multiply one-digit whole numbers by multiples of 10 in the range 10–90 (e.g., 9 × 80, 5 × 60) using strategies based on place value and properties of operations.

Standards Crosswalk

Second Grade
Number and Operations in Base Ten
Understand place value.
- Understand that the digits of a three-digit number represent amounts of hundreds, tens, and ones.
- 100 can be thought of as a bundle of 10 tens or a "hundred".
- The multiples of 100 (through 900) refer to 1–9 hundreds, 0 tens, and 0 ones.
- Count within 1000.
- Skip-count by 5s, 10s, and 100s.
- Read and write numbers to 1000 using numerals, number names, and expanded form.
- Use >, =, and < to compare two three-digit numbers.

Use place value understanding and properties of operations to add and subtract.
- Fluently add and subtract within 100.
- Add up to four two-digit numbers.
- Add and subtract within 1000, relating the strategies used to a written method.
- Mentally add or subtract 10 or 100 to or from a given number 100–900.
- Explain why addition and subtraction strategies work.

Fourth Grade
Number and Operations in Base Ten
Generalize place value understanding for multi-digit whole numbers.
- Recognize that each place value is 10 times larger than the one to its right.
- Read and write multi-digit whole numbers using numerals, words, or expanded form.
- Compare two multi-digit numbers using >, =, and <.
- Round multi-digit whole numbers to any place.

Use place value understanding and properties of operations to perform multi-digit arithmetic.
- Fluently add and subtract multi-digit whole numbers.
- Multiply whole numbers of up to four digits by a one-digit number, and two two-digit numbers.
- Find whole-number quotients and remainders with up to four-digit dividends and one-digit divisors.

3.NBT.A.1

3.NBT.A.2

3.NBT.A.3

3.NBT.A.1				
3.NBT.A.2				
3.NBT.A.3				

3.NBT.A.1				
3.NBT.A.2				
3.NBT.A.3				

Number and Operations—Fractions

3.NF.A.1 Understand a fraction $1/b$ as the quantity formed by 1 part when a whole is partitioned into b equal parts; understand a fraction a/b as the quantity formed by a parts of size $1/b$.

3.NF.A.2 Understand a fraction as a number on the number line; represent fractions on a number line diagram.

3.NF.A.2a Represent a fraction $1/b$ on a number line diagram by defining the interval from 0 to 1 as the whole and partitioning it into b equal parts. Recognize that each part has size $1/b$ and that the endpoint of the part based at 0 locates the number $1/b$ on the number line.

3.NF.A.2b Represent a fraction a/b on a number line diagram by marking off a lengths $1/b$ from 0. Recognize that the resulting interval has size a/b and that its endpoint locates the number a/b on the number line.

3.NF.A.3 Explain equivalence of fractions in special cases, and compare fractions by reasoning about their size.

3.NF.A.3a Understand two fractions as equivalent (equal) if they are the same size, or the same point on a number line.

3.NF.A.3b Recognize and generate simple equivalent fractions, e.g., $1/2 = 2/4$, $4/6 = 2/3$. Explain why the fractions are equivalent, e.g., by using a visual fraction model.

3.NF.A.3c Express whole numbers as fractions, and recognize fractions that are equivalent to whole numbers. Examples: Express 3 in the form $3 = 3/1$; recognize that $6/1 = 6$; locate $4/4$ and 1 at the same point of a number line diagram.

3.NF.A.3d Compare two fractions with the same numerator or the same denominator by reasoning about their size. Recognize that comparisons are valid only when the two fractions refer to the same whole. Record the results of comparisons with the symbols >, =, or <, and justify the conclusions, e.g., by using a visual fraction model.

Note: Grade 3 expectations in this domain are limited to fractions with denominators 2, 3, 4, 6, and 8.

Standards Crosswalk

Second Grade

*The Number and Operations—Fractions domain begins in third grade.

Geometry

Reason with shapes and their attributes.

- Partition a rectangle into rows and columns of same-size squares and count to find the total number of them.
- Partition circles and rectangles into two, three, or four equal shares, using the words *halves*, *thirds*, *half of*, *a fourth of*, etc., to describe them.
- Describe a divided whole as two halves, three thirds, four fourths.
- Recognize that equal shares of identical wholes may not have the same shape.

Fourth Grade

Number and Operations—Fractions

Extend understanding of fraction equivalence and ordering.

- Recognize and form equivalent fractions.
- Compare two fractions with different numerators and different denominators using >, =, and <.

Build fractions from unit fractions by applying and extending previous understandings of operations on whole numbers.

- Understand fractions with numerators greater than one as sums of unit fractions $1/b$.
- Add and subtract mixed numbers with like denominators.
- Multiply a fraction by a whole number.
- Understand fractions with numerators greater than one as multiples of the unit fraction $1/b$.

Understand decimal notation for fractions, and compare decimal fractions.

- Rename and add fractions with denominators of 10 and 100.
- Rewrite fractions with denominators of 10 or 100 as decimals.
- Compare two decimals to hundredths using >, =, or <.

3.NF.A.1

3.NF.A.2

3.NF.A.3

3.NF.A.1

3.NF.A.2

3.NF.A.3

26

© Carson-Dellosa CD-104802

3.NF.A.1

3.NF.A.2

3.NF.A.3

Measurement and Data

3.MD.A.1

Tell and write time to the nearest minute and measure time intervals in minutes. Solve word problems involving addition and subtraction of time intervals in minutes, e.g., by representing the problem on a number line diagram.

3.MD.A.2

Measure and estimate liquid volumes and masses of objects using standard units of grams (g), kilograms (kg), and liters (l). Add, subtract, multiply, or divide to solve one-step word problems involving masses or volumes that are given in the same units, e.g., by using drawings (such as a beaker with a measurement scale) to represent the problem.

3.MD.B.3

Draw a scaled picture graph and a scaled bar graph to represent a data set with several categories. Solve one- and two-step "how many more" and "how many less" problems using information presented in scaled bar graphs. *For example, draw a bar graph in which each square in the bar graph might represent 5 pets.*

3.MD.B.4

Generate measurement data by measuring lengths using rulers marked with halves and fourths of an inch. Show the data by making a line plot, where the horizontal scale is marked off in appropriate units—whole numbers, halves, or quarters.

3.MD.C.5

Recognize area as an attribute of plane figures and understand concepts of area measurement.
- 3.MD.C.5a A square with side length 1 unit, called "a unit square," is said to have "one square unit" of area, and can be used to measure area.
- 3.MD.C.5b A plane figure which can be covered without gaps or overlaps by n unit squares is said to have an area of n square units.

3.MD.C.6

Measure areas by counting unit squares (square cm, square m, square in, square ft, and improvised units). *(Excludes compound units and finding the geometric volume of a container.)*

3.MD.C.7

Relate area to the operations of multiplication and addition.
- 3.MD.C.7a Find the area of a rectangle with whole-number side lengths by tiling it, and show that the area is the same as would be found by multiplying the side lengths.
- 3.MD.C.7b Multiply side lengths to find areas of rectangles with whole-number side lengths in the context of solving real world and mathematical problems, and represent whole-number products as rectangular areas in mathematical reasoning.
- 3.MD.C.7c Use tiling to show in a concrete case that the area of a rectangle with whole-number side lengths a and $b + c$ is the sum of $a \times b$ and $a \times c$. Use area models to represent the distributive property in mathematical reasoning.
- 3.MD.C.7d Recognize area as additive. Find areas of rectilinear figures by decomposing them into non-overlapping rectangles and adding the areas of the non-overlapping parts, applying this technique to solve real world problems.

3.MD.D.8

Solve real world and mathematical problems involving perimeters of polygons, including finding the perimeter given the side lengths, finding an unknown side length, and exhibiting rectangles with the same perimeter and different areas or with the same area and different perimeters.

Standards Crosswalk

Second Grade
Measurement and Data
Measure and estimate lengths in standard units.
- Measure the length of an object by selecting and using appropriate tools.
- Measure the length of an object using two different length units and relate the measurements to the units used.
- Estimate lengths using units of inches, feet, centimeters, and meters.
- Measure to determine how much longer one object is than another.

Relate addition and subtraction to length.
- Use addition and subtraction within 100 to solve word problems involving lengths given in the same units.
- Represent whole numbers as lengths from 0 on a number line and represent whole-number sums and differences within 100 on a number line.

Work with time and money.
- Tell and write time from analog and digital clocks to the nearest five minutes, using am and pm.
- Solve word problems involving dollar bills, quarters, dimes, nickels, and pennies, using $ and ¢ symbols appropriately.

Represent and interpret data.
- Measure objects and represent measurements on a line plot (to the nearest whole unit).
- Draw a picture graph and a bar graph (with single-unit scales) to represent up to four categories.
- Solve simple addition, subtraction, and comparison problems using information given in a graph.

Fourth Grade
Measurement and Data
Solve problems involving measurement and conversion of measurements from a larger unit to a smaller unit.
- Know relative sizes of measurement units within one system of units including km, m, cm; kg, g; lb., oz.; l, mL; hr., min., sec.
- Convert measurements within a measurement system (from a larger unit to a smaller unit).
- Use the four operations to solve measurement word problems.
- Use the area and perimeter formulas for rectangles.

Represent and interpret data.
- Create line plots displaying fractions (1/2, 1/4, 1/8).
- Solve problems involving addition and subtraction of data presented on line plots

Geometric measurement: understand concepts of angle and measure angles.
- Recognize angles are formed by two rays with the same endpoint.
- Understand that an angle is measured in degrees of a circle.
- Measure and draw whole-number angles using a protractor.
- Understand that the sum of an angle's parts is equal to the whole angle.
- Solve addition and subtraction problems to find unknown angles.

3.MD.A.1																	
3.MD.A.2																	
3.MD.B.3																	
3.MD.B.4																	
3.MD.C.5																	
3.M.C.6																	
3.MD.C.7																	
3.MD.D.8																	

3.MD.A.1																	
3.MD.A.2																	
3.MD.B.3																	
3.MD.B.4																	
3.MD.C.5																	
3.MD.C.6																	
3.MD.C.7																	
3.MD.D.8																	

3.MD.A.1																				
3.MD.A.2																				
3.MD.B.3																				
3.MD.B.4																				
3.MD.C.5																				
3.MD.C.6																				
3.MD.C.7																				
3.MD.D.8																				

Geometry

Second Grade
Geometry
Reason with shapes and their attributes.
- Recognize and draw shapes with specific attributes.
- Identify triangles, quadrilaterals, pentagons, hexagons, and cubes.
- Partition a rectangle into rows and columns of same-size squares and count to find the total number of them.
- Partition circles and rectangles into two, three, or four equal shares, using the words *halves, thirds, half of, a fourth of*, etc., to describe them.
- Describe a divided whole as two halves, three thirds, four fourths.
- Recognize that equal shares of identical wholes may not have the same shape.

Fourth Grade
Geometry
Draw and identify lines and angles, and classify shapes by properties of their lines and angles.
- Draw and identify points, lines, line segments, rays, angles, and perpendicular and parallel lines in two-dimensional figures.
- Classify polygons by the types of angles and lines used to form them.
- Recognize that lines of symmetry divide a shape into matching parts.
- Identify symmetrical shapes.
- Draw lines of symmetry.

3.G.A.1

3.G.A.2

3.G.A.1

3.G.A.2

3.G.A.1

3.G.A.2

Reading Standards for Literature

RL.3.1 Ask and answer questions to demonstrate understanding of a text, referring explicitly to the text as the basis for the answers.

RL.3.2 Recount stories, including fables, folktales, and myths from diverse cultures; determine the central message, lesson, or moral and explain how it is conveyed through key details in the text.

RL.3.3 Describe characters in a story (e.g., their traits, motivations, or feelings) and explain how their actions contribute to the sequence of events.

RL.3.4 Determine the meaning of words and phrases as they are used in a text, distinguishing literal from nonliteral language.

RL.3.5 Refer to parts of stories, dramas, and poems when writing or speaking about a text, using terms such as chapter, scene, and stanza; describe how each successive part builds on earlier sections.

RL.3.6 Distinguish their own point of view from that of the narrator or those of the characters.

RL.3.7 Explain how specific aspects of a text's illustrations contribute to what is conveyed by the words in a story (e.g., create mood, emphasize aspects of a character or setting).

RL.3.8 (not applicable to literature)

RL.3.9 Compare and contrast the themes, settings, and plots of stories written by the same author about the same or similar characters (e.g., in books from a series).

RL.3.10 By the end of the year, read and comprehend literature, including stories, dramas, and poetry, at the high end of the grades 2–3 text complexity band independently and proficiently.

Standards Crosswalk

Second Grade
Reading: Literature
Key Ideas and Details
- Ask and answer such questions as *who*, *what*, *where*, *when*, *why*, and *how* about key details in a text.
- Recount stories, including fables and folktales from diverse cultures, and determine their central messages, lessons, or morals.
- Describe how characters in a story respond to major events and challenges.

Craft and Structure
- Describe how words and phrases supply rhythm and meaning in a story, poem, or song.
- Describe the overall structure of a story.
- Understand the purpose of a story's beginning and ending.
- Acknowledge differences in the points of view of characters.
- Use different voices for each character when reading dialogue aloud.

Integration of Knowledge and Ideas
- Use information from illustrations and words in text to demonstrate understanding of its characters, setting, or plot.
- Compare and contrast two or more versions of the same story by different authors or from different cultures.

Range of Reading and Level of Text Complexity
- By the end of the year, proficiently read and comprehend literature in the grades 2–3 text complexity band.

Fourth Grade
Reading: Literature
Key Ideas and Details
- Refer to text details and examples when explaining text and drawing inferences.
- Use text details to determine a theme of a story, drama, or poem.
- Summarize a text.
- Describe a character, setting, or event in depth using specific details from text.

Craft and Structure
- Determine the meaning of words and phrases in a text, including those alluding to mythological characters.
- Explain major differences between poems, drama, and prose, and refer to the structural elements of poetry and drama when writing or speaking about a text.
- Compare and contrast the points of view of different stories.
- Know the difference between first- and third-person point of view.

Integration of Knowledge and Ideas
- Make connections between the text of a story or drama and a visual or oral presentation of the text.
- Compare and contrast similar themes and topics and patterns of events in stories, myths, and traditional literature from different cultures.

Range of Reading and Level of Text Complexity
- By the end of the year, proficiently read and comprehend literature in the grades 4–5 text complexity band.

RL.3.1																				
RL.3.2																				
RL.3.3																				
RL.3.4																				
RL.3.5																				
RL.3.6																				
RL.3.7																				
RL.3.9																				
RL.3.10																				

48

RL.3.1					
RL.3.2					
RL.3.3					
RL.3.4					
RL.3.5					
RL.3.6					
RL.3.7					
RL.3.9					
RL.3.10					

RL.3.1																				
RL.3.2																				
RL.3.3																				
RL.3.4																				
RL.3.5																				
RL.3.6																				
RL.3.7																				
RL.3.9																				
RL.3.10																				

52

Reading Standards for Informational Text

RI.3.1 Ask and answer questions to demonstrate understanding of a text, referring explicitly to the text as the basis for the answers.

RI.3.2 Determine the main idea of a text; recount the key details and explain how they support the main idea.

RI.3.3 Describe the relationship between a series of historical events, scientific ideas or concepts, or steps in technical procedures in a text, using language that pertains to time, sequence, and cause/effect.

RI.3.4 Determine the meaning of general academic and domain-specific words and phrases in a text relevant to a *grade 3 topic or subject area*.

RI.3.5 Use text features and search tools (e.g., key words, sidebars, hyperlinks) to locate information relevant to a given topic efficiently.

RI.3.6 Distinguish their own point of view from that of the author of a text.

RI.3.7 Use information gained from illustrations (e.g., maps, photographs) and the words in a text to demonstrate understanding of the text (e.g., where, when, why, and how key events occur).

RI.3.8 Describe the logical connection between particular sentences and paragraphs in a text (e.g., comparison, cause/effect, first/second/third in a sequence).

RI.3.9 Compare and contrast the most important points and key details presented in two texts on the same topic.

RI.3.10 By the end of the year, read and comprehend informational texts, including history/social studies, science, and technical texts, at the high end of the grades 2–3 text complexity band independently and proficiently.

Standards Crosswalk

Second Grade
Reading: Informational Text

Key Ideas and Details
- Ask and answer questions such as *who*, *what*, *where*, *when*, *why*, and *how* about key details in a text.
- Identify the main topic of a multi-paragraph text and the focus of specific paragraphs.
- Describe the connection between a series of historical events, scientific ideas or concepts, or steps in technical procedures in a text.

Craft and Structure
- Determine the meaning of words and phrases in a text.
- Use text features (captions, bold print, subheadings, glossaries, indexes, electronic menus, icons) to locate information.
- Identify the main purpose of a text, including the author's purpose.

Integration of Knowledge and Ideas
- Explain how specific images contribute to and clarify a text.
- Describe how reasons support specific points made in a text.
- Compare and contrast key points presented by two texts on the same topic.

Reading and Level of Text Complexity
- By the end of the year, read and comprehend informational texts in the grades 2-3 complexity band.

Fourth Grade
Reading: Informational Text

Key Ideas and Details
- Refer to text details and examples when explaining text and drawing inferences.
- Determine the main idea of a text using key details.
- Summarize a text.
- Explain events, procedures, ideas, or concepts in a historical, scientific, or technical text, including what happened and why, based on specific information.
- Determine the meaning of general academic and domain-specific words or phrases in a grade 4 text.
- Describe the overall structure of events, ideas, concepts, or information in a text.
- Compare and contrast a firsthand and secondhand account of the same event or topic, including the focus and the information provided.

Integration of Knowledge and Ideas
- Interpret information presented visually, orally, or quantitatively and explain how it contributes to an understanding of the text.
- Explain how an author uses reasons and evidence to support text points.
- Integrate information from two texts on the same topic to write or speak knowledgeably about the subject.

Range of Reading and Level of Text Complexity
- By the end of year, read and comprehend informational texts in the grades 4–5 text complexity band proficiently.

RI.3.1							
RI.3.2							
RI.3.3							
RI.3.4							
RI.3.5							
RI.3.6							
RI.3.7							
RI.3.8							
RI.3.9							
RI.3.10							

56

© Carson-Dellosa CD-104802

RI.3.1																				
RI.3.2																				
RI.3.3																				
RI.3.4																				
RI.3.5																				
RI.3.6																				
RI.3.7																				
RI.3.8																				
RI.3.9																				
RI.3.10																				

RI.3.1																				
RI.3.2																				
RI.3.3																				
RI.3.4																				
RI.3.5																				
RI.3.6																				
RI.3.7																				
RI.3.8																				
RI.3.9																				
RI.3.10																				

RF.3.1	(Ends in grade 1)
RF.3.2	(Ends in grade 1)
RF.3.3	Know and apply grade-level phonics and word analysis skills in decoding words. RF.3.3a Identify and know the meaning of the most common prefixes and derivational suffixes. RF.3.3b Decode words with common Latin suffixes. RF.3.3c Decode multisyllable words. RF.3.3d Read grade-appropriate irregularly spelled words.
RF.3.4	Read with sufficient accuracy and fluency to support comprehension. RF.3.4a Read grade-level text with purpose and understanding. RF.3.4b Read grade-level prose and poetry orally with accuracy, appropriate rate, and expression on successive readings. RF.3.4c Use context to confirm or self-correct word recognition and understanding, rereading as necessary.

Standards Crosswalk

Second Grade
Reading: Foundational Skills
Print Concepts and Phonological Awareness end in first grade.
Phonics and Word Recognition
- Know and apply grade-level phonics and word analysis skills.
- Identify long and short vowels in regularly spelled one-syllable words.
- Know spelling-sound correspondences for additional common vowel teams.
- Decode regularly spelled two-syllable words with long vowels.
- Decode words with common prefixes and suffixes.
- Identify words with inconsistent but common spelling-sound correspondences.
- Recognize and read grade-appropriate irregularly spelled words.

Fluency
- Read with sufficient accuracy and fluency to support comprehension.
- Read grade-level text with purpose and understanding.
- Read grade-level text orally with accuracy, appropriate rate, and expression on successive readings.
- Use context and rereading to confirm or self-correct word recognition and understanding.

Fifth Grade
Reading: Foundational Skills
Phonics and Word Recognition
- Know and apply grade-level phonics and word analysis skills in decoding words.
- Use combined knowledge of all letter-sound correspondences, syllabication patterns, and roots and affixes to accurately read unfamiliar multisyllabic words.

Fluency
- Read with sufficient accuracy and fluency to support comprehension.
- Read grade-level text with purpose and understanding.
- Read grade-level prose and poetry orally with accuracy, appropriate rate, and expression on successive readings.
- Use context and rereading to confirm or self-correct word recognition and understanding.

RF.3.3

RF.3.4

RF.3.3

RF.3.4

RF.3.3																		

RF.3.4																		

Writing

W.3.1 Write opinion pieces on topics or texts, supporting a point of view with reasons.
- W.3.1a Introduce the topic or text they are writing about, state an opinion, and create an organizational structure that lists reasons.
- W.3.1b Provide reasons that support the opinion.
- W.3.1c Use linking words and phrases (e.g., *because, therefore, since, for example*) to connect opinion and reasons.
- W.3.1d Provide a concluding statement or section.

W.3.2 Write informative/explanatory texts to examine a topic and convey ideas and information clearly.
- W.3.2a Introduce a topic and group related information together; include illustrations when useful to aiding comprehension.
- W.3.2b Develop the topic with facts, definitions, and details.
- W.3.2c Use linking words and phrases (e.g., *also, another, and, more, but)* to connect ideas within categories of information.
- W.3.2d Provide a concluding statement or section.

W.3.3 Write narratives to develop real or imagined experiences or events using effective technique, descriptive details, and clear event sequences.
- W.3.3a Establish a situation and introduce a narrator and/or characters; organize an event sequence that unfolds naturally.
- W.3.3b Use dialogue and descriptions of actions, thoughts, and feelings to develop experiences and events or show the response of characters to situations.
- W.3.3c Use temporal words and phrases to signal event order.
- W.3.3d Provide a sense of closure.

W.3.4 With guidance and support from adults, produce writing in which the development and organization are appropriate to task and purpose. (Grade-specific expectations for writing types are defined in standards 1–3 above.)

W.3.5 With guidance and support from peers and adults, develop and strengthen writing as needed by planning, revising, and editing. (Editing for conventions should demonstrate command of Language standards 1–3 up to and including grade 3.)

W.3.6 With guidance and support from adults, use technology to produce and publish writing (using keyboarding skills) as well as to interact and collaborate with others.

W.3.7 Conduct short research projects that build knowledge about a topic.

W.3.8 Recall information from experiences or gather information from print and digital sources; take brief notes on sources and sort evidence into provided categories.

W.3.9 (begins in grade 4)

W.3.10 Write routinely over extended time frames (time for research, reflection, and revision) and shorter time frames (a single sitting or a day or two) for a range of discipline-specific tasks, purposes, and audiences.

Standards Crosswalk

Second Grade
Writing
Text Types and Purposes
- Write opinion pieces that introduce a topic or book, state an opinion, supply reasons to support the opinion, use linking words, and provide a concluding statement or section.
- Write informative/explanatory texts that introduce a topic, use facts and definitions to develop points, and provide a concluding statement or section.
- Write narratives that recount a well-elaborated event or short sequence of events; include details to describe actions, thoughts, and feelings; use temporal words to signal event order; and provide a sense of closure.

Production and Distribution of Writing
With guidance and support:
- Focus on a topic and strengthen writing as needed by revising and editing.
- Use a variety of digital tools to produce and publish writing, including in collaboration with peers.

Research to Build and Present Knowledge
- Participate in shared research and writing projects.
- Recall information from experiences or gather information from provided sources to answer a question.

Range of Writing begins in grade 3.

Fourth Grade
Writing
Text Types and Purposes
- Write opinion pieces, supporting a point of view with reasons and information.
- Introduce the topic or text clearly, state an opinion, and use an organized structure to group related ideas; provide reasons supported by facts and details; use linking words and phrases to connect opinion and reasons; provide a conclusion related to the opinion.
- Write informative/explanatory texts to examine a topic and convey ideas and information clearly.
- Introduce a topic clearly; group related information in paragraphs and sections; and include formatting, illustrations, and multimedia when useful; develop a topic with facts, definitions, concrete details, quotations, and other relevant information; use linking words and phrases to connect ideas; provide a concluding statement or section related to the information presented.
- Write real or imaginary narratives using effective technique, details, and clear sequences.
- Establish a situation and introduce a narrator and/or characters; organize a natural event sequence; uses dialogue, and description to develop experiences, events, and characters' responses; use concrete words, phrases, and sensory details to convey experiences and events precisely; provide a conclusion that follows from the events.

Production and Distribution of Writing
- Produce clear and coherent writing with development and organization that is appropriate to task and purpose.
- With guidance and support, develop and strengthen writing as needed by planning, revising, and editing.
- With some guidance and support, use technology to produce and publish writing as well as to interact and collaborate with others.
- Demonstrate sufficient keyboarding skills to type at least one page in a sitting.

Research to Build and Present Knowledge
- Conduct short research projects that build knowledge about a topic's various aspects.
- Recall relevant information from experiences or gather information from print and digital sources.
- Take notes, categorize information, and provide a list of sources.
- Draw evidence from texts to support analysis, reflection, and research.

Range of Writing
- Write routinely over extended and shorter time frames for a range of discipline-specific tasks, purposes, and audiences.

W.3.1																			
W.3.2																			
W.3.3																			
W.3.4																			
W.3.5																			
W.3.6																			
W.3.7																			
W.3.8																			
W.3.10																			

72

© Carson-Dellosa CD-104802

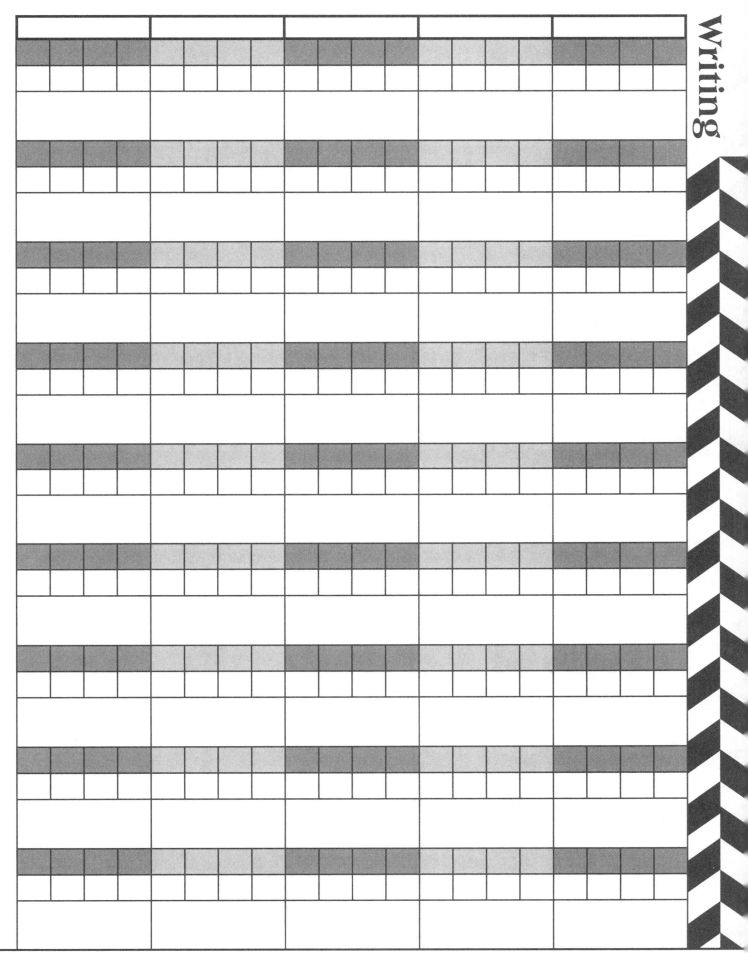

W.3.1					
W.3.2					
W.3.3					
W.3.4					
W.3.5					
W.3.6					
W.3.7					
W.3.8					
W.3.10					

© Carson-Dellosa CD-104802

W.3.1																				
W.3.2																				
W.3.3																				
W.3.4																				
W.3.5																				
W.3.6																				
W.3.7																				
W.3.8																				
W.3.10																				

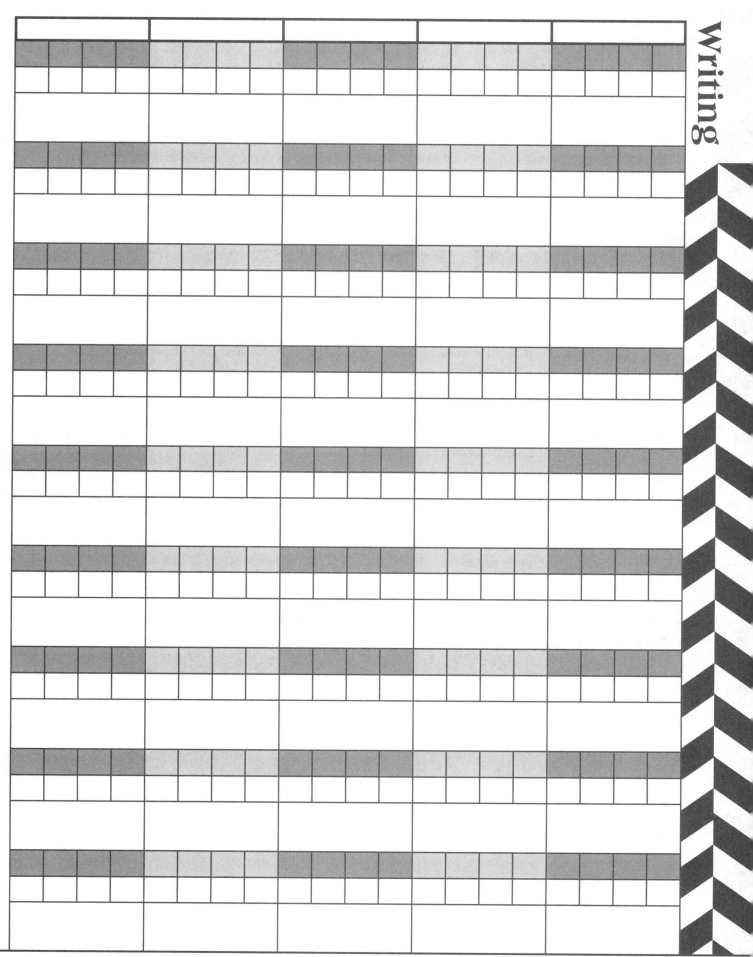

Speaking and Listening Standards

SL.3.1

Engage effectively in a range of collaborative discussions (one-on-one, in groups, and teacher-led) with diverse partners on *grade 3 topics and texts*, building on others' ideas and expressing their own clearly.

SL.3.1a   Come to discussions prepared, having read or studied required material; explicitly draw on that preparation and other information known about the topic to explore ideas under discussion.

SL.3.1b   Follow agreed-upon rules for discussions (e.g., gaining the floor in respectful ways, listening to others with care, speaking one at a time about the topics and texts under discussion).

SL.3.1c   Ask questions to check understanding of information presented, stay on topic, and link their comments to the remarks of others.

SL.3.1d   Explain their own ideas and understanding in light of the discussion.

SL.3.2

Determine the main ideas and supporting details of a text read aloud or information presented in diverse media and formats, including visually, quantitatively, and orally.

SL.3.3

Ask and answer questions about information from a speaker, offering appropriate elaboration and detail.

SL.3.4

Report on a topic or text, tell a story, or recount an experience with appropriate facts and relevant, descriptive details, speaking clearly at an understandable pace.

SL.3.5

Create engaging audio recordings of stories or poems that demonstrate fluid reading at an understandable pace; add visual displays when appropriate to emphasize or enhance certain facts or details.

SL.3.6

Speak in complete sentences when appropriate to task and situation in order to provide requested detail or clarification.

_____
_____
_____
_____
_____
_____
_____
_____

© Carson-Dellosa CD-104802

Standards Crosswalk

Second Grade

Speaking and Listening

Comprehension and Collaboration

- Participate in group discussions about grade-appropriate topics and texts.
- Follow agreed upon discussion rules.
- Comment on the remarks of others, and ask for clarification if needed.
- Recount or describe key ideas or details from a text or other channels of information.
- Ask and answer questions about a presentation to clarify comprehension, gather more information, or deepen understanding.

Presentation of Knowledge and Ideas

- Audibly and coherently tell a story or recount an experience with appropriate facts and relevant, descriptive details.
- Create audio recordings of stories or poems.
- Add drawings or other visual displays when appropriate.
- Produce complete sentences to provide requested detail or clarification.

Fourth Grade

Speaking and Listening

Comprehension and Collaboration

- Actively participate in collaborative discussions on grade 4 topics and texts, building on others' ideas and expressing their own clearly.
- Prepare for discussions, using that preparation to explore ideas under discussion.
- Follow agreed-upon rules for discussions and carry out assigned roles.
- Ask and answer questions to clarify information presented, contribute to the conversation, and link comments to others' remarks.
- Explain their ideas and understanding in light of the discussion.
- Paraphrase a text read aloud or other channels of information.
- Identify the reasons and evidence a speaker provides to support particular points.

Presentation of Knowledge and Ideas

- Report on a topic or text, tell a story, or recount an experience in an organized manner, with appropriate facts and descriptive details.
- Speak clearly at an understandable pace.
- Add audio and visual displays when appropriate.
- Differentiate between contexts that need formal and informal English.

SL.3.1																				
SL.3.2																				
SL.3.3																				
SL.3.4																				
SL.3.5																				
SL.3.6																				

SL.3.1																				
SL.3.2																				
SL.3.3																				
SL.3.4																				
SL.3.5																				
SL.3.6																				

83

SL.3.1																			
SL.3.2																			
SL.3.3																			
SL.3.4																			
SL.3.5																			
SL.3.6																			

Language Standards

Demonstrate command of the conventions of standard English grammar and usage when writing or speaking.
- L.3.1a   Explain the function of nouns, pronouns, verbs, adjectives, and adverbs in general and their functions in particular sentences.
- L.3.1b   Form and use regular and irregular plural nouns.
- L.3.1c   Use abstract nouns (e.g., *childhood*).
- L.3.1d   Form and use regular and irregular verbs.
- L.3.1e   Form and use the simple (e.g., *I walked*; *I walk*; *I will walk*) verb tenses.
- L.3.1f   Ensure subject-verb and pronoun-antecedent agreement.
- L.3.1g   Form and use comparative and superlative adjectives and adverbs, and choose between them depending on what is to be modified.
- L.3.1h   Use coordinating and subordinating conjunctions.
- L.3.1i   Produce simple, compound, and complex sentences.

Demonstrate command of the conventions of standard English capitalization, punctuation, and spelling when writing.
- L.3.2a   Capitalize appropriate words in titles.
- L.3.2b   Use commas in addresses.
- L.3.2c   Use commas and quotation marks in dialogue.
- L.3.2d   Form and use possessives.
- L.3.2e   Use conventional spelling for high-frequency and other studied words and for adding suffixes to base words (e.g., *sitting*, *smiled*, *cries*, *happiness*).
- L.3.2f   Use spelling patterns and generalizations (e.g., *word families*, *position-based spellings*, *syllable patterns*, *ending rules*, *meaningful word parts*) in writing words.
- L.3.2g   Consult reference materials, including beginning dictionaries, as needed to check and correct spellings.

Use knowledge of language and its conventions when writing, speaking, reading, or listening.
- L.3.3a   Choose words and phrases for effect.
- L.3.3b   Recognize and observe differences between the conventions of spoken and written standard English.

Determine or clarify the meaning of unknown and multiple-meaning word and phrases based on *grade 3 reading and content*, choosing flexibly from a range of strategies.
- L.3.4a   Use sentence-level context as a clue to the meaning of a word or phrase.
- L.3.4b   Determine the meaning of the new word formed when a known affix is added to a known word (e.g., *agreeable/disagreeable*, *comfortable/uncomfortable*, *care/careless*, *heat/preheat*).
- L.3.4c   Use a known root word as a clue to the meaning of an unknown word with the same root (e.g., *company*, *companion*).
- L.3.4d   Use glossaries or beginning dictionaries, both print and digital, to determine or clarify the precise meaning of key words and phrases.

Demonstrate understanding of figurative language, word relationships and nuances in word meanings.
- L.3.5a   Distinguish the literal and nonliteral meanings of words and phrases in context (e.g., *take steps*).
- L.3.5b   Identify real-life connections between words and their use (e.g., describe people who are *friendly* or *helpful*).
- L.3.5c   Distinguish shades of meaning among related words that describe states of mind or degrees of certainty (e.g., *knew*, *believed*, *suspected*, *heard*, *wondered*).

Acquire and use accurately grade-appropriate conversational, general academic, and domain-specific words and phrases, including those that signal spatial and temporal relationships (e.g., *After dinner that night we went looking for them*).

Standards Crosswalk

Second grade
Language

Conventions of Standard English
- Use collective nouns; form and use frequently occurring irregular plural nouns; use reflexive pronouns; form and use the past tense of common irregular verbs; use adjectives and adverbs appropriately.
- Produce, expand, and rearrange complete simple and compound sentences.
- Capitalize holidays, product names, and geographic names; use commas in greetings and closings of letters; use apostrophes to form contractions and frequently occurring possessives.
- Generalize learned spelling patterns when writing words; consult reference materials as needed to check and correct spellings.

Knowledge of Language
- Compare formal and informal uses of English.

Vocabulary Acquisition and Use
- Use sentence-level context as a clue to the meaning of a word or phrase.
- Determine meaning when a known prefix is added to a known word; use a known root word to determine an unknown word with the same root; use knowledge of individual words to predict the meaning of compound words; use glossaries and dictionaries to determine the meaning of new words.
- Identify real-world connections between words and their uses.
- Distinguish shades of meaning among related verbs and related adjectives.
- Use words and phrases (including descriptive adjectives and adverbs) acquired through conversations, reading and being read to, and responding to texts.

Fourth Grade
Language

Conventions of Standard English
- Use relative pronouns and relative adverbs; form and use progressive verb tenses; use modal auxiliaries to convey various conditions; order adjectives within sentences according to conventional patterns; form and use prepositional phrases.
- Produce complete sentences and correct fragments and run-on sentences.
- Correctly use frequently confused words.
- Use correct capitalization, punctuation, and spelling when writing.
- Use correct punctuation when writing quotations and dialogue; use a comma before a coordinating conjunction in a compound sentence.
- Spell grade-appropriate words correctly, consulting references as needed.

Knowledge of Language
- Choose words and phrases to convey ideas precisely.
- Choose punctuation for effect.
- Choose when to use formal or informal language.

Vocabulary Acquisition and Use
- Determine or clarify the meanings of unknown and multiple-meaning words and phrases.
- Use context as a clue to the meaning of a word or phrase; use Greek and Latin prefixes, suffixes, and roots to understand unfamiliar words; consult reference materials to find the pronunciation and meaning of words and phrases.
- Understand figurative language, word relationships, and nuances in word meanings; explain the meaning of simple similes and metaphors in context; recognize and explain the meaning of common idioms, adages, and proverbs.
- Use antonyms and synonyms to better understand words.
- Learn and use academic and subject-specific vocabulary, including words that signal precise actions, emotions, or states of being.

L.3.1																			
L.3.2																			
L.3.3																			
L.3.4																			
L.3.5																			
L.3.6																			

	L.3.1																		

L.3.1

L.3.2

L.3.3

L.3.4

L.3.5

L.3.6

L.3.1																				
L.3.2																				
L.3.3																				
L.3.4																				
L.3.5																				
L.3.6																				

Name _____   **Date** _____

Standard _____

_____

_____

_____

_____

_____

Notes